BLUBBER

Katie Greenall

methuen | drama
LONDON • NEW YORK • OXFORD • NEW DELHI • SYDNEY

METHUEN DRAMA
Bloomsbury Publishing Plc, 50 Bedford Square, London, WC1B 3DP, UK
Bloomsbury Publishing Inc, 1359 Broadway, New York, NY 10018, USA
Bloomsbury Publishing Ireland, 29 Earlsfort Terrace, Dublin 2, D02 AY28, Ireland

BLOOMSBURY, METHUEN DRAMA and the Methuen Drama logo are trademarks of Bloomsbury Publishing Plc.

First published in Great Britain 2026

Cover photography by Claudia Legge

A catalogue record for this book is available from the British Library.

Library of Congress Control Number: 2026933031

ISBN: PB: 978-1-3506-3220-2
ePDF: 978-1-3506-3221-9
eBook: 978-1-3506-3222-6

Series: Modern Plays

Typeset by Mark Heslington Ltd, Scarborough, North Yorkshire

For product safety related questions contact productsafety@bloomsbury.com.

To find out more about our authors and books visit www.bloomsbury.com and sign up for our newsletters.

BLUBBER

Written and Performed by Katie Greenall
Director and Dramaturg - Rafaella Marcus
Designer - Hazel Low
Lighting Designer - Lauren Woodhead
Sound Design and Composition - AJ Turner
Sound Design and Composition - Anna Clock
Movement Director - Phao May
Video Designer - Rachel Sampley
Show Parent - Jen Smethurst
Production and Stage Manager - Stacey Sandford
Producer - Daisy Hale, The Hale
Associate Producer - Sean Brooks, The Hale
Assistant Producer - Olivia Seward, The Hale
PA and Support Worker - Riss Obolensky, The Hale
Artwork Photography - Claudia Legge
Production Photography - Michael Aiden Photography

Seed Commissioned by Marlborough Productions and supported by MAST, Cambridge Junction, Arts Depot and VAULT.

With thanks to Hackney Showroom, Brixton House, house southeast theatre network, Roundhouse, Barbican, Jenni Jackson, Al Orange, Chloe Stally-Gibson, Han Sayles, Wet Mess, Kimberley Capero, Harry Elletson, Mann Bros, Sian Morrell, Karma.

BLUBBER was first performed at TechCube0, Summerhall, Edinburgh Festival Fringe from Tuesday 13 - Monday 26 August 2024.

Katie Greenall - Writer & Performer

Katie Greenall (she/they) is a director, theatre maker & writer living in NE London. She specialises in new writing, solo autobiographical work and working with Young People and Communities.

They are currently the Associate Director at the Royal Exchange Theatre. Previously she was the Associate Director at the Bush Theatre, where they established the Bush Young Companies. Their directing credits include: *Make Me Feel* (Bush Theatre), *Communion* (Bush Theatre); *We All Know How this Ends* (Theatre Royal Stratford East); *As We Face The Sun* (Offie nominated, Bush Theatre); *Pass It On* (Bush Theatre); *Here, Here, Here* (Theatre Royal Stratford East); *Anthem* (Bush Theatre); *Back Up!* (Bush Theatre). She was also the Associate Director on *Barcelona* (Duke of York's Theatre).

As a writer, Katie was a member of the Poetry Collective at the Roundhouse and a Resident Artist at the Roundhouse in 2018-19. She was part of the Soho Theatre Writer's Lab programme, long-listed Channel 4 Screenwriting Course in 2021 and a member of VAULT Five. In 2020, she was runner up in Evening Standard Future Theatre Fund for theatre making and in 2024 was on the shortlist for the Popcorn Award. They have also appeared on radio and several podcasts, including BBC's Women's Hour & The Guilty Feminist, as well as writing from the Metro Online, Refinery29 & Bustle.

Alongside *BLUBBER*, Katie also made *FATTY FAT FAT*, a solo show about living in a fat body. It won the VAULTS Origins Award for Outstanding New Work in 2019 and following this, completed a sold out 5* run at Edinburgh Festival Fringe. In Spring 2020, *FATTY FAT FAT* was due to head out on a tour of England & Wales, and its final performances were in Soho Theatre's main house in September 2021.

www.katiegreenall.com

Rafaella Marcus - Director & Dramaturg

Rafaella Marcus (she/they) is a director, writer and dramaturg.

As director, they were the Runner Up of the JMK Award in 2021. Recent work includes *Bury the Dead* (Finborough); *Richard II* (RADA); *Stop Kiss* (Above The Stag); *Crave* (Bunker Theatre); *I Have a Mouth and I Will Scream* (VAULT Festival – People's Choice Award winner); *The Wild Party* (The Hope Theatre).

Work as Associate and Assistant Director includes: *Blithe Spirit* (Harold Pinter Theatre) and *Emilia* (Vaudeville Theatre).

Work as writer includes her debut play *Sap* (Paines Plough Roundabout/National Tour/Soho Theatre), for which she won the Off-West End Award for Most Promising New Playwright.

Hazel Low - Designer

Credits include: *Animal Farm* (Tobacco Factory, Bristol); *Make Me Feel*, *Pause/Rewind*, *As We Face The Sun*, *Pass It On* (Bush Theatre); *Playfight* (Bristol Old Vic, Belgrade Coventry, Soho Theatre); *The Crucible* (egg theatre, Bath); *The Glorious French Revolution (or why sometimes it takes a guillotine to get anything done)* (New Diorama Theatre); *The Legend of Ned Ludd* (Everyman Theatre, Liverpool); *succession theme is my ringtone* (Rose Theatre); *Tiger* (Omnibus Theatre); *Bonfire* (Derby Theatre, Sheffield Theatre, Nonsuch Studios); *Who Killed my Father* (co-design with Blythe Brett) (Camden People's Theatre and Scottish Tour); *Bogeyman* (Pleasance Queendome).

As Assistant/Associate: *I, Joan* (Shakespeare's Globe); *Paradise Now* (Bush Theatre); *Blood Show and Monster Show* (Cambridge Junction); *The Winston Machine* (New Diorama); *Beautiful Thing* (Stratford East).

Hazel is also an Associate Lecturer on BA Theatre Design at UAL Wimbledon College of Arts.

Lauren Woodhead - Lighting Designer

Credits include: *Main Character Energy* (Soho Theatre); *The Sun Does Shine* (Hackney Empire); *The Second Woman, the fabric with Colour Vogue Ball, Of the Cut, AI, The new tomorrow* (Young Vic); *BURGERZ* (Co-Design, Hackney Showroom, UK and International tour); *If you love me this might hurt* (Camden People's Theatre); *FATTY FAT FAT* (UK tour); *Really real TEENZ* (The Yard theatre); *Man Muck* (The Etcetera Theatre).

Theatre as Associate Lighting Designer includes: *Britannicus* (Lyric Hammersmith); *FITTER* (Soho theatre); *The crown dual* (Wilton's Music Hall).

Theatre as Assistant Lighting Designer includes: *Jesus Christ Superstar, As You Like It* (Open Air, Regents Park); *Jubilee* (Royal Exchange theatre & Lyric Hammersmith).

AJ Turner - Sound Design and Composition

AJ Turner is a composer, sound designer and multi-instrumentalist working across contemporary theatre, live art and experimental music based in London. Their practice centres on the raw, visceral affectivity of sound in performance, creating and collaborating on interdisciplinary projects through an intersectional feminist, disabled, queer lens.

Their work in critically acclaimed theatre productions has toured internationally and across the UK, seen at venues including The Almeida, Battersea Arts Centre, Schaubühne (Berlin), Carriageworks (Sydney), Frascati (Amsterdam), Arken (Copenhagen), and Soho Playhouse (New York). In their experimental music work they have been commissioned by organisations including the London Sinfonietta, Philharmonia Orchestra and Spitalfields Music. They were a Bang on a Can (New York) Composer Fellow in 2018, and a London Sinfonietta Writing the Future Composer from 2020 - 2022.

Anna Clock - Sound Design and Composition

Anna Clock (they/them) is an artist, composer and musician. Their work spans theatre, film, radio, installation, written texts and live music. Their practice is centred on ways of listening, and challenging audiences to listen to each other, and their world, in new ways. They play the cello and also cut hair.

They have presented work at theatres, galleries and venues including Barbican, The Royal Court Theatre, Wellcome Collection, Shakespeare's Globe, Royal Exchange Theatre, The Albany, Lyric Hammersmith, Soho Theatre, V & A Museum, Museum of Science and Industry, Copeland Gallery (UK), Project Arts Centre, Cooper Gallery, Gate Theatre (IRL), Times Square Arts, Irish Arts Centre, UC San Diego (USA), Mainz Staatstheater, Dresden Staatsschauspiel (GER), and a range of site specific locations including basements, cemeteries and a raft on a pond.

Their audio works have been played on Radio 4, Radio 3, Resonance FM, Earth FM and RTE Lyric radio.

Their compositions have been played by ensembles such as RTE Contempo Quartet, Tonnta, New Dublin Voices, Kirkos Ensemble, Node Ensemble, Dulciana, Gamelan Nua and Téada Orchestra, and as a musician they have collaborated with Ailbhe Nic Oireachtaigh, Woven Skull, Hozier, David Lacey, Gavin Prior, David Turpin, Emma O'Reilly and others.

In 2020-22 they consulted on an independent research project into medical listening and telehealth supported by The Cleveland Clinic and Columbia University, and they have an ongoing collaborative research project with neuro-ethicist Lauren Sankary around sound, headphone space, gender and vulnerability.

Their work is often participatory and they have run workshops, lectured and taught in the UK, Ireland, Germany, the USA, Colombia, and online.

Phao May - Movement Director

Phao is a Movement Director, Choreographer, Theatre Director, Intimacy Director, and Facilitator. Her work blends physicality, theatricality, and narrative to create bold, expressive storytelling that provokes, empowers, and connects.

With over a decade in the arts, Phao has collaborated with leading venues, companies and schools, including The Bush Theatre, Soho Theatre, The Roundhouse, National Youth Theatre, and Guildhall School of Music and Drama.

Phao's creative background spans stage, screen, cabaret, music videos, commercials, and community projects, with training that includes an MA in Movement: Directing and Teaching from The Royal Central School of Speech and Drama, an Acting Foundation from RADA, and advanced burlesque training at The Cheek Of It! School of Burlesque and Cabaret.

Whether creating movement for theatre, choreographing for music videos, or leading workshops, Phao's process balances rigour with play, creating spaces where performers can take risks, push boundaries, and bring their full creative selves to the work.

Rachel Sampley - Video Designer

Rachel Sampley is a multimedia artist. She has a background in lighting and video design including creative captions. She loves bold colorful playful typography and hopes that people find power, solidarity, and emotional connection when seeing the words of their community curated together.

Credits include: *Argos Archives* (Omnibus), *Welcome Home* (Soho Theatre), *Ar Barrier(s)* (National Theatre), *Perfect Show for Rachel* (The Barbican), *The Great Gatsby* (Immersive Everywhere), *The Suspicions of Mr Whicher* (The Watermill Theatre), *Bossy* (Zoo Co; Southbank Centre) and *Cassie and the Lights* (59E59, Off Broadway, NY). *Opal Fruits* (Bristol Old Vic, Pleasance Edinburgh) (Immersive LDN: Seoul, Korea: Theatre Clwyd), *Wreckage* (Turbine Theatre), and *Breeding* (King's Head Theatre - Offie nominated for Lighting Design}

She has an MA in Advanced Theatre Practice from the Royal Central School of Speech and Drama.

Jen Smethurst - Show Parent

Jen Smethurst is a Practices of Care & Project Planning Consultant, Well-being Practitioner, Show Parent, Access Support Person & General Vibes Manager. They specialise in working with intersectionally-marginalised people in creative & performance contexts.

For more information about what this means and to book them for jobs, visit their website: jensmethurst.com

The Hale

The Hale is a London-based arts producing company specialising in experimental, socially-engaged work that is not restricted by form. The Hale was founded in 2021 by Daisy Hale, Creative Director.

We exist to produce and develop artists who have been traditionally ostracised from mainstream spaces with a focus on Queer, Trans, Global Majority & Learning Disabled & Neurodivergent identities.

We describe ourselves as your cultural nightclub; in any room anything could be happening. We make shows, parties, cabarets, workshops, digital happenings, cultural events that can happen anywhere, anytime.

We are just as interested in art as protest as art for fun - often they can be the same. Our work prioritises joy over trauma, looking for the fun in the mundane and using populism as an access point for deeper conversation with a broad audience about socio-political issues.

Our work is countercultural, care focused and transparent. Often we work in models of co-creation and non-hierarchy.

It is important to us to consistently share our process to both keep an archive of marginalised work, but also to demystify the practice of producing. We advocate for better producer development and access into producing as a career.

Alongside producing we do fundraising, access support, workshop facilitation & disability equality training.

www.the-hale.com

BLUBBER

For my Body,
I am forever indebted to you

IN THE BEGINNING

We see **Katie** *reach for a story inside of herself. It's like she is speaking to us from a pulpit. Perhaps there is an urgency for it to emerge or maybe it slips out softly.*

In the beginning, there was Katie, and there was Body. Katie and Body were best friends. They grew and learnt and played together. They rolled in amongst the soft rolls of each other, trying to navigate their wild and expansive world. In the beginning, Katie and Body were infinite with possibilities.

But as time passed, it became harder and harder to keep the harsh whispers of the world from coming between them. Things between Katie and Body grew more difficult. Katie and Body grew in different ways; Body got bigger in places Katie wished were smaller and Katie grew away from Body.

There was a river of aching between Katie and Body and no way to get across.

Body begins to leave **Katie**. *There is a disconnect between what we hear and see.*

Body didn't know how to be with Katie anymore – every step felt loaded with a thousand moments of heaviness. Body was ancient with hurting and Katie didn't know how to help. So, she didn't.

And so, one night, whilst Katie slept too deeply, Body made a choice. A choice so deeply painful but quiet at the same time – it was time for Body to say goodbye to Katie.

Body took one last look at the person it had called home, and then with heartbreak, hurting and deep relief, Body slipped into the ocean of night.

Katie *and Body are separated.*

A shift.

One of the first times I ever called myself fat was on stage. For the last seven years, my relationship with my body has mainly been a professional one. Transactional. Exploitative even?

I ended the last show that I made with the line 'I want my body back'. I feel further away from my body now than I ever have before. I often feel like I am talking about my body like its not there, like I've lost it along the way. Publicly, privately, intimately. I feel like I'm speaking about what it needs, advocating for its basic rights or defending its existence, all without it really acknowledging that its *my* body that I am talking about.

I am resolutely and absolutely pro-fat. But when you're bombarded with uncomfortable chairs, government-funded hate campaigns and people you love telling you being fat is ok for you but not what they want for themselves, you have to create a bit of distance in order to not to succumb to it all. I've sacrificed my relationship and developed this numbness with my body to protect my politics, I think.

Sometimes, I wish I'd kept my body just for me.

There is a change. Maybe it is subtle or maybe it is obvious – regardless, it is monumental.

I want to mythologise this story of me and my body.

I want to make myself mythical in order to feel more real.

What if I showed you my belly (figuratively)? The softest most vulnerable parts of me in the hope I/we could maybe find something new?

So we begin . . .

In the beginning . . .
In the beginning . . .

In the beginning
I was the whole world.

MY BODY JUST FOR ME

Katie I have been trying to think about the times when I have felt most connected to my body. I would love to say on stage – because it feels like the right answer for any self-respecting artiste. But really it's:

1. When I'm in water, not like swimming up and down but like diving, rolling and doing handstands. I am outstanding at handstands in the pool.
2. When I'm singing really loud and/or really high
3. And perhaps my favourite, when I'm sitting on a bench at night looking out across a body of water, smoking a single cigarette.

Recently, the most I've *felt* my body is through heartbreak. An ancient aching in my chest that reminded me it was still there. I don't want my body to be a graveyard, punctuated only by the pain of grief and longing.

A shift.

One night, Katie felt so far away from herself she crept out alone into the night. These days, loneliness was the closest she got to rest, and the emptiness of the night helped her forget the missing.

Katie found herself sitting on the wooden slats of her midnight timeshare and looked out across the water, as every pore of her saluted the skyline in a goosebump. As Katie took in her surroundings, she saw a message etched into the sky. Katie allowed her eyes to soften around the edges of the letters, it simply read . . . goodbye. It was then Katie realised Body was gone.

For a while Katie allowed herself to imagine Body on its own adventure. She saw it dancing up the mountains she'd never had enough breath to climb. She heard it screaming until its tired lungs were so brutally empty that it felt like the freedom. She saw Body diving off the ramparts of the world, being caught by the bluest water and after swimming to the farthest corners being rocked to sleep by the waves. She saw Body feasting, pouring banquets into each hand and swallowing them whole.

More
and more
and more
and more
and more
and more
and more,

Instead of the less that she and Body had come to know.

Katie had to do something, feel something again. So, Katie decided she was going to get her Body back. And the only place she knew to start looking for Body, was the water.

SYNCHRO

There is a change.

Sound enters the space, it's 'Beautiful' by Christina Aguilera but with a thumping beat beneath it. **Katie** *appears on stage in a flamboyance – maybe accompanied by sequins, waltzing waters and Esther Williams-esque kitsch. It is high camp.* **Katie** *begins to move to the music. Her movements are inspired by and mimic those in synchronised swimming. She skulls, rolls, flips, kicks and glides.*

At climactic intervals throughout the song **Katie** *stops to speak directly to the audience. Maybe while she speaks, she holds a ridiculous pose from her routine, or maybe she allows herself to drop the pretence completely. The first time she speaks she says:*

Katie This is not a show about synchronised swimming.

Katie *begins to move again. Perhaps it is even more ridiculous than before.*

But the plan was to make a show about synchro. Maybe that's the reason why you're here? So . . . this is 'THE SYNCHRO BIT'.

Katie *moves again – perhaps it is even more ridiculous than before.*

Sorry - the plan was to make a show about synchronised swimming. Inspired by the all-fat synchro group from the 90s called the Padded Lilies. I did start to learn – and I want to show you, I want to give the people what they want . . . .

There is a climax of the movement, accompanied by a small shower from a handful of very small water pistols.

Perhaps there is a small bow, there is definitely applause.

Katie *collects herself.*

The first thing you learn in synchro is sculling. Sculling is where you make a sort of dish shape with your hands, put them by your sides and use them to propel you. And then there's the 'eggbeater', which is where you rotate your legs like a whisk and it helps lift you out of the water. Like this . . .

She demonstrates. Maybe the audience join in. Maybe they try it out together.

And I was quite good at it. Because my body, for one of the first times in my life, has a tangible advantage – the superpower of floating.

Ok so it's not really a superpower, it's science and I have an A level in science so it felt appropriate to use it at some point. It's quite dry to try and explain buoyance, but the main thing you need to know is the swimmer always wants to float and will float unless it experiences some kind of external force. Then it will sink.

There are three things that affect your ability to float: muscle mass, bone density and fat. Bone and muscle are heavier than water so they sink. Whereas fat is light, so it floats.

Over time, the word fat has become synonymous with things like heavy, solid and dense – but that simply isn't true. Scientifically fat is light, it floats. Which means, so am I. Or at least I have the potential to be. And in the right context I am.

At first synchro did all the things I wanted it to. It gave me space to think about how to make sense of my body. So, I started to think about how to make sense of my body alongside science – something I am rarely afforded the privilege of being able to do without it being linked to a death sentence – and I was reminded of aquatic ape theory.

Aquatic ape theory is a widely defunct evolutionary theory, focused on the idea that we might have evolved from sea mammals, rather than apes. Built around the ideas, such as: that we have less hair on us than apes from our being streamline in the sea, we can speak because we know how to hold and release our breath from diving into the water, we walk upright from wading and, most importantly for me, our fat is spread in a layer around our body like a whale, rather than just around its organs.

No matter how you think the world came to be, it's very unlikely this is evolutionary fact, but what if it was true for me?

What if I had always been designed to be like this?
What if my fatness is a unique evolutionary gift?
What if fat people came from the sea?

I wanted to find a version of my own genesis, that acknowledged my fatness, rather than constantly painting me as at risk of extinction.

So, in the beginning . . .
In the beginning . . .

Katie *speaks to us from her pulpit again, addressing the congregation.*

In the beginning, maybe I came from the water.
Maybe I came from the rivers, oceans, lakes and seas.
Maybe I came from the streams, the rain, the puddles and the tears.

Maybe I emerged out of the water,
bulbous body naked,
free from the layer of hair that coats the outside edges of my cousins.
Instead, my skin as naked as my sisters:
the walruses, manatees and whales.

My body that wasn't born scared to drown,
instead is seemingly designed to glide, float and swim.

Maybe it's because I came from the water that I can speak.
I can hold and release my breath,
unlike other creatures,
because I have the memory of having to take deep dives of air.
– Maybe I've always had to breathe in, to ensure I am able to eat.

And maybe it's because I came from the water that I am fat –
My body carved from blubber.
Whilst my relatives collect fat around the inside wall of their bodies,
Protecting their precious organs,
My sisters from the seas, their fat is spread out in a layer
Adorning their perimeters.
Evolved and adapted to achieve the perfect complete fatness.

Every part of my skin is lined with fat too,
Sometimes many walls thick.
It is apparently biologically impossible for any other primate to be as fat as I am now
But the walruses, the manatees, the whales and I swim on.

Katie *is grounded again.*

I first embarked on learning synchro when I heard about people like me, doing this thing I'd always wanted to do. There was this sense of possibility that synchro could be the container for all the things I needed it to be. Be this fun thing that was accessible to my body, whilst also providing a space to tangibly connect with it. But the problem was, synchro couldn't really see itself like that.

There was a moment before our Christmas show, where we were all poolside marking through our routine (a festive mega-mix of 'Judas' by Lady Gaga followed by 'Born This Way') all half-naked, adorned in tinsel with nose clips – as if it was the Olympics or something. The hire before us was starting to run over and so we were increasingly irate. We were ready to divebomb in protest when we realised it was a group of adults getting baptised.

I think I was also looking for some kind of baptism. A washing away of the shame I had held about my body through doing something new. But that wasn't how it was set up to be. It was still measured by the same familiar metrics: how fast you can be, how far you can bend and how full you can fill your lungs.

So, I stopped going. Partly because adults with hobbies take things very seriously and it's quite intense. And partly because I was full of this muted disappointment that synchro wasn't the thing I wanted it to be. There was no rage or dramatic exit, in fact I kept on saying I was going to come back, in the slightly too-active group chat. But I didn't, for lots of reasons, and the main one being, I just couldn't bring myself to. I didn't want to subject myself to this disappointment.

A shift.

This show really is a different show to what I thought I was making.

This is a show I genuinely thought I'd never make, but we're here now.

WHALE

There is a stark aloneness here as **Katie** *is lost in the depths of herself, but equally at her strongest. This moment should feel unarguable with.*

Katie Katie was perched amongst the waves, right up until she wasn't. Suddenly, she felt the air change around her, it was denser and darker, like she was disappearing down the plug hole in the centre of the Earth. But it was over almost as quickly as it began, as Katie landed with a thick thud.

Katie sat wide awake in this dark squashy space and took a deep sticky breath. She felt her breath reverberate deeply around her. Katie took in its softness, hearing nothing but a dull rhythmic thumping which seemed to be coming from every direction.

All Katie knew was that she had no idea where she was, where she was going or, more importantly, where Body was. So, she sat in this perpetual aloneness, lost, and in complete despair.

A shift.

I don't think I realised how isolating it would be to renounce everything I've ever known about my body and seek to completely reframe my understanding of myself – because that's what I have had to do over the last seven years. I never considered what it might take to make peace with the fact I will probably never not be fat. To abandon the want to be thin, especially when that was your life's purpose for so long. To hold this secret understanding of how the hatred against your body has been constructed over generations and is perpetuated by people you love. For so much of what you do and are to be considered 'radical', 'revolutionary' or 'brave'.

Whenever I have experienced fat community and solidarity, it has either been incidental or I've had to make it myself. I think I thought by starting synchro I might find fat community – but that wasn't the case.

It's so incredible lonely holding all this by myself.

//

Katie *summons the whale song from buried deep within its rib cage.* **Katie** *joins in with the sound that surrounds her. It is huge, encompassing and reverberates off every surface in the space. The audience should feel it bouncing off their organs as it roars. A gut-wrenching beautiful sound. By the end the singing has changed from one steeped in despair to that of some kind of recognition.*

Katie was inside the fattest body on earth.
Katie was inside the body of a whale.

She listened to the whale's deep supernatural echoes, as they reverberated through fat and water.

As she sat in the shadow of the holy spires of the whale's rib bones, she realised that she had never challenged or doubted the strength, grace or gift of whales and their fatness. A whale's fatness that is so special and scared, it has its own name: blubber.

But the whale belongs in the water – its enormous body makes sense in the expansive oceans. Katie thought about Body and couldn't think of a time where it felt they had made sense anywhere. Where they had been able to move through the world like the whale moved through the ocean.

And worse Katie realised her own ability to care for Body had run out, so no wonder it wanted to leave her behind. She felt herself flood with shame at the realisation she wasn't enough, even for her own flesh.

It's building.

All of a sudden, the walls of the whale's soft kingdom shook with a guttural thunder. Katie begun to be bounced about like a floundering fish, flipping and folding, being caught only by a net of muscles and sinew. She became submerged, swirling in a mix of spittle and sea water.

Something erupts. It should feel like the tectonic plates of the story are hurtling towards each other.

Silence.

The whale had spat her back out.

THE REUNION

Katie Katie landed on the shore of an island. Gone was the familiar softness of the ocean. Instead she lay in her heaviness rolling in the wake of the waves as they crashed into a handshake with the sand. As she felt the fingers of the ocean's carefulness fall away from her for the last time, she was struck by how hollow and barren it felt to be back on dry land.

Katie looked to the sky, looking for something to guide her in this hopelessness. Another message perhaps? She looked up to the sand dunes in the distance and –

– and saw Body, cloaked by the horizon.

Katie looked at Body and Body looked at Katie. She arose slowly, achingly close to the moment she voyaged across the world for. The world had pulled them apart, but now was offering them a chance to come back together – a single drop of hope floating between them.

The potential of this moment is held briefly.

A change.

Maybe in a thousand years time, Katie and Body will run to each other across the sand like long lost-lovers, with a romantic rain storm of tears and a congregation of 'I'm sorry's and 'I love you's' buried into each other's cheeks. But in reality, this reunion was quiet, tentative and uncertain.

The sun beat down like the fork on the side of a glass, beckoning a speech. Katie took a breath, a breath that cleared the sky of clouds in the hope they would soak up the sadness in her soul. Katie opened her mouth . . .

There is a moment full of a sad possibility. These two things that had been separated for so long are in touching distance; it should feel like Michelangelo's The Creation of Adam. *So close, yet so far.*

(Recorded.) Katie opened her mouth, but nothing came out.

The last drip of faith dries up.

The stage feels empty, stark and arid, with the world we've come to know disappearing in front of us. The story of Katie and Body lies littered across the floor.

CREATION

We are in a different world now.

Katie *feels small on the stage. Maybe she cleans up some mess or maybe she makes more. It's live and almost too real.*

Everything feels different now.

Katie I think I want this show to be the last show I make about fatness. It's getting too hard and I'm worried I've done too much damage. I have holes in my shoulders from carrying this all on my chest.

There is stillness.

I have remained resolute throughout my life. I am an independent person, but really I think I just wanted to prepare myself for what felt inevitable – living my life alone. You're so conditioned to believe that fatness makes you so unworthy of care and value, that when I made the choice to stay fat, I think I felt like I made a commitment to being alone forever, and since then having been trying to prepare myself for that.

But what's hard is in the making of this show and during this time in my life, I've realised that I can't exist in isolation like that. None of us can. I need you.

I need you to grant me my full humanity.

I made myself a whole universe so I could talk about the grief and loneliness I had been feeling in my own body, with the optimism it might help me find an answer or a way through. But even in my stories, I'm stuck somewhere between not wanting to hate my body, but not being able to give it everything it deserves either. At the end of it all, the care.

That really scares me. I'm scared that I might spend the rest of my life feeling like this.

I don't want to keep telling stories where I'm the only person in them. And so, I have been thinking about what I can do, what we might be able to do together.

I invite you to be the water, to help me build the world where I make sense. Be the water that lifts me and gives me lightness – for me and for all of you too.

Katie *looks at the audience. It's a long stare equally balanced somewhere between hopefulness and hopelessness. She gathers any objects she might need.*

So, will you help me? With a baptism of sorts. Something from all of us, to bodies like mine. If you would like to, a few of you can come on stage and join me.

Katie *invites the audience to come down and wash/bathe/cleanse her. There are six set roles, which are:*

- *Washing of arms × 2*
- *Washing of legs × 2*
- *Washing of face*
- *Washing/brushing hair*

Each is to be done with honesty and reflection, anointing **Katie**'*s soft body with care. It should feel tender, intimate even.*

Once the washing is complete, **Katie** *invites those people to take their seats again.*

After this, **Katie** *hums the beautiful whale song or maybe wails it. This moment is tender; there is a vulnerability even. We are reminded of her humanity in this moment. We are reminded that she is not part of a story, she is a real human being.*

There is some kind of hope, an offer of a new beginning.

REBIRTH

We return to the familiar world of the quest. It feels a bit like a relief. But something feels different.

A loaded quiet hangs.

In the beginning, there was Katie, and there was Body.

Katie and Body weren't best friends. But they grew and learnt and played together. They rolled in amongst the soft rolls of each other, trying to navigate their wild and expansive world.

In this new beginning, Katie and Body weren't infinite with possibilities. They were tired, lonely and scared – but held together delicately, by the possibility of the care that might be possible for them.

Blackout.

THE END

ACKNOWLEDGEMENTS

Thank you to house, Arts Council England, arts depot, Cambridge Junction, Battersea Arts Centre, Roundhouse, Marlborough Productions, VAULT Festival, the Barbican and MAST.

To the whole *BLUBBER* team who have been ever patient, generous and wise throughout this journey.

To Raf, without whom this show would not be what it is today. Thank you for your trust, care and insight.

To Dais and Sean at The Hale, who never gave up on me or this show. I am so grateful for all of your hard work and dedication.

To my friends and family, for their unwavering support, love and belief. It is a privilege to grow alongside you and be loved by you.

And as always, thank you to the fat activists and artists (especially the members of the Fat Performance Network) for continuing to inspire, provoke and advocate for work like this and bodies like mine.

www.ingramcontent.com/pod-product-compliance
Lightning Source LLC
LaVergne TN
LVHW052343100826
845147LV00021B/1170

* 9 7 8 1 3 5 0 6 3 2 2 0 2 *